32 PAIRS OF GLOVES

a monologue

Stanley Rutherford

BROADWAY PLAY PUBLISHING INC
New York
www.broadwayplaypublishing.com
info@broadwayplaypublishing.com

32 PAIRS OF GLOVES
© Copyright 2020 Stanley Rutherford

First edition: December 2020
I S B N: 978-0-88145-880-0

Book design: Marie Donovan
Page make-up: Adobe InDesign
Typeface: Palatino

32 PAIRS OF GLOVES was originally presented at the Throckmorton Theatre in Mill Valley, California, in June 2012. The cast and creative contributor were:

WILLA .... Amy Resnick

Director ....Hal Gelb

CHARACTER & SETTING

WILLA. *She is of a certain age. She wears a rather provocative short-skirted ensemble. She wears very bright red lipstick, lots of it. She is a major media "life-style" personality, currently in eclipse. She is magnificently poised, erect, very disciplined, precise, and extravagant of movement.*

A long row of old mismatched chests of drawers, different heights and styles, each painted a different color of blue. There is also a scattering of seven old wooden chairs, also shades of blue.

(WILLA *stands in front of the drawers, addressing the audience.*)

WILLA: The issue has been ill defined.

The issue has been co-opted by the sensationalist media.

The issue has been...what is the issue?

This is the question.

(*She moves and poses.*)

For years I've been planning to recover the sofa.

And I've looked...

Have you looked lately for fabric?

I can't find any fabric.

Fabric is the issue.

There's fabric, but there's not...it's just...the *usual* fabric, brocades, chintzes, sort-of rayon-ey...I can't stand anything that looks too..."designed", too..."new".

The issue is "newness".

The issue is what is "newness" and should we care.

The issue is the fact that the sensationalist media has claimed ownership of "newness" and turned "newness" into a commodity, and if we don't possess the "new" we are marginalized.

(*She moves and poses.*)

I shall open a drawer.

(She opens a drawer and looks inside.)

I shall close the drawer.

(She closes the drawer.)

I shall open another drawer.

(She opens another drawer and looks inside.)

I shall close the drawer.

(She closes the drawer.)

So finally I decided to keep the old ratty, wine- and grease-stained upholstery, and I threw a remnant of something nostalgic over it, and now it's all quite romantic, nicely lived-in, and everything is just fine.

I shall move a chair.

(She crosses and moves one of the chairs, pauses, studies it, moves it again, studies it, then moves and poses.)

So many of you have been writing me about your decorating issues...

...and how you have fear of decorating and the expense of decorating and the concern that you'll select the wrong color or the wrong fabric or the wrong combination of textures and treatments and you'll be unhappy with what you've selected and you'll be judged by what you've selected, and it's very stressful, very very stressful.

Stress is the issue.

Stress is the predominant issue.

There has always been stress, but now there is more stress, and the stress is the result of the sensationalist media that panders to the consumer's need for newness, need for controversy, need for outrage, and so the sensationalist media blows up the horrifying blood-drenched detail until it becomes the whole picture, and we walk around with the horrifying

blood-drenched detail and think that it is the whole
picture, but it is *not* the whole picture, we don't know
the whole picture, and even if we knew the whole
picture, what in the hell would we do?

(She takes a lipstick from her pocket and applies it efficiently, expertly.)

I shall open a drawer.

(She opens a drawer.)

I shall close the drawer.

(She closes the drawer.)

I shall move a chair.

(She moves a chair and positions it.)

I shall move another chair.

(She moves another chair and positions it.)

You've been cutting pictures out of magazines, haven't
you…

I understand…

…subscribing to magazines, purchasing magazines
at the check-out, casually lifting magazines from
the dental office, I know, I understand…cutting out
pages from the *House Beautiful* at the gymnasium, and
you've created a file, haven't you, of ripped-out, cut-
out pictures of the kitchen, bath, foyer, loft bedroom,
living room, and now you have boxes of old pictures,
and at night as you try to drift off to slumberland your
head is awash with images of kitchens and bathrooms
and foyers and loft bedrooms and exciting yet low-
cost window treatments, and your so-called "spare"
room is now piled with the boxes of creased and
yellowed and greasy-fingered pictures of kitchens and
bathrooms and foyers and loft bedrooms and exciting
yet low-cost window treatments, and your life is sheer
hell.

I understand. I know. I care.

I too used to cut out pictures and save them, and as I have told you, I obsessively organized them and fantasized about them, and after the divorce, I decided that something had to be done, and I took all the boxes of pictures and gave them to my dear, dear friend Denise.

I shall move a chair.

(She crosses to a chair, moves the chair and studies it, then moves it closer to the audience.)

I shall now sit.

(She sits on the chair and crosses one leg over the other.)

I feel so very close to you.

(She re-crosses her legs.)

And I know that you feel so very close to me.

(She re-crosses her legs again.)

And we've been through so much together, and we know that in our hearts we are so, so, so very very much alike...tastes, beliefs, dental hygiene issues, anxieties, hair and lower back issues...

And over the years I've been reaching out and you've been reaching out, and it's so big out there, isn't it, so frightening, so unfriendly, so overwhelming, so mysterious...

Yet we know that we understand one another and trust one another, and tonight we have come together to open our hearts, and feel the love between us, and share our stories and our love of beauty and the refined, tasteful lifestyle...and our commitment to locally grown, low-fat, low-calorie, whole grain, non-genetically altered foods.

(She re-crosses her legs.)

I have not wanted to discuss the divorce.

(She re-crosses her legs again.)

And I know you wondered about the divorce and I truly wanted to tell you about the divorce but it was all so very very difficult because so few knew that Summerfield and I were married in the first place. We hadn't informed the general public about the marriage, and so when the divorce occurred, and it was inevitable, I didn't want to address the issue, but then the sensationalist, smut-obsessed media published the photograph of me on the courthouse steps in tears, with the screaming headline: "Summerfield dumps Willa!!!"

I shall open a drawer.

(She stands, crosses, and opens a drawer. She pulls out newspaper clippings. She starts to show them to the audience, but then stops, upset.)

No, I am not going to show these to you.

Hideously unkind articles, hurtful, untruthful, lies…

You devote your life to helping people…in simple ways, I've tried to help, tried to instruct and cast a loving ray of light into the darkness…and they build you up, they celebrate, they adulate, and then they destroy.

(She puts the clippings back in the drawer and closes it.)

I shall open a drawer

(She opens another drawer and takes out a stack of magazines and shows them to the audience.)

Here I've kept the cover stories, the pictures of me when the pathologically lurid media loved me, when people wanted to interview me, ask me about my life; What is Willa thinking? What is Willa doing now? How is Willa styling her hair? Is she still wearing that fabulously shocking red lipstick?... *(Indicating)* Here is the eight-page color spread about Summerfield's and my love-filled holiday in the 14th century convent-turned-luxury-spa on the Amalfi coast. *(Indicating)* Here is the at-home interview about how I'd transformed my living room, and created a romantic outdoor seating area using every day materials and matte-finish blue paint. *(Indicating)* Here is the how-to photo essay about the fabulously festive holiday table settings I created with do-it-yourself gold-leaf nut cups and flower baskets, and fun little marzipan squirrels and pheasants nestled amidst boughs of pine and spruce.

(She puts the magazines back in the drawer and closes it, then turns to the audience.)

So many of you have written such wonderful heartfelt notes...

...outpourings of understanding and compassion about my legal and marital dilemmas...

...loving commentaries about how you've personally benefitted from my tips on creative budgeting strategies, dealing with mold and mildew, and grateful appreciations for my campaign to promote a common-sense approach to maintaining a diet rich in polyphenols and flavonoids to support a healthy, robust lifestyle.

And you've been asking me questions...so many many lovely questions...

...I love your questions...wonderful, caring questions, and not just about decorating and household management issues, grooming, nutrition and financial issues, but *personal* issues, *real* issues, like:

Am I dating again?

Am I still interested in calligraphy?

Has my bout with a misdiagnosed bi-polar condition improved?

Do I have a last name? Have I always been just "Willa?"

It touches me deeply that you have these questions... such sensitive, lovely, inquisitive people...caring people...

I shall open a drawer.

(She stands, crosses and opens a drawer, looks inside, lets out a prolonged, blood-curdling scream, slams the drawer shut, collects herself breathing deeply, using her body to secure the drawer, holding it firmly shut.)

There are terrible things. Unspeakable. Horrifying. Tragic.

(She turns and opens the drawer again, looks inside, lets out a prolonged, blood-curdling scream, slams the drawer shut, collects herself, then turns to the audience.)

We cannot hide.

This is the issue.

We cannot escape and I tried to deny this fact, and I lived in a dream world of bourgeois mindlessness, repotting my plants, stenciling grape vine tendrils around my windows and doors, and then the Summerfield affair...the incriminating photos... the tax fraud allegations...the sensationalist media's venomous examination of every aspect of my life, including the weight gain, the weight loss, the weight gain, the liposuction, the chin lift, the brow lift, the breast enhancement, the horrifying loss of my hair following my ill-advised attempt to create shimmering highlights with allegedly non-toxic, made-in-China bleaching agents.

It caused me a great deal of anguish...

...and it caused my mother, now deceased, a great deal of anguish... *(She tears up, fights back the tears, then...)* You would have liked my mother...lovely woman. Pisces. Lovely. Kind. Anorexic. Quietly, tastefully alcoholic. Divorced at an early age from my father, the claims adjuster, leaving her alone, every night alone, drinking, watching T V shows with wild animals, the predators, the prey, the lame, the malnourished... *(She tears up again)* I'm sorry, please forgive me...

(She dries her eyes, pulls herself together, adjusts her posture, then...)

I shall move a chair.

(She crosses to a chair and moves it.)

I shall sit.

(She sits, and crosses her legs.)

I shall move the chair again.

(She stands and moves the chair and studies it.)

I shall reposition the chair.

(She repositions the chair and sits, crosses her legs, applies lipstick again, then re-crosses her legs.)

(Initiating a radiant inviting smile) I'm so moved that you've come here tonight. We know that you have choices, you could have gone elsewhere...the cinema, the...oh, I don't know, the bowling...so many things, the P B S, the Netflix, the karaoke...

And yet you've come here...to be with me...and provide your loving support.

You're looking lovely, I just want to say that, absolutely lovely...so filled with health, just look at you...marvelous...all that water you drink, marvelous...all those sun salutations, marvelous... broccoli, green tea...it's so wonderful how you strive to better yourselves, develop new interests, seek to understand the new developments in nutrition and creative household finance, and sustain a sense of emotional equilibrium despite the relentless efforts of the media to keep us in a constant state of anxiety, horror, and disbelief.

I shall open a drawer.

(She stands, crosses, opens a drawer, looks inside.)

Here is where I keep my vitamins and nutritional supplements...the fish oil, the vitamin D, various amino acids that promote brain health and weight loss, the grape seed extract, the co-enzyme Q-10...the essentials...

(She closes the drawer, then opens another.)

Here is where I keep my skin care lotions, moisturizers, sunscreens, and personal lubricants...organization I find is so so so important, it helps to provide a feeling of tranquility and control in a world of discord and chaos.

(She closes the drawer, then opens another.)

And here is the costume I wore when I was in the May Day pageant in the seventh grade. I was a butterfly...

(She pulls out a butterfly costume and holds it up)

...Isn't it lovely? ...My mother made it, silken wings, a blaze of color, and I flew around, free, beautiful, it was one of my most wonderful moments.

(She closes the drawer, then opens another.)

And this is where I keep Miss Patsy Cline...

(She sings:)

I fall to pieces,
Each time I see you again...

I just love Patsy Cline, my mother loved Patsy Cline, the honesty of the woman, the *truth* of the woman, the struggles, the car crash, the plane crash, the men...I loved her...

(She closes the drawer, then opens another.)

And this is...oh my God...I wondered what happened to that...oh, my God, this is so fabulous...a marvelous totally candid at-home photo of me and Julia Child...

I just adored Julia, marvelous fun, and she invited me over to her beautiful brilliantly messy kitchen to show me how to make puff pastry. And so we started drinking a lovely Bordeaux, and Julia took out about nine pounds of butter from the fridge, and we drank more wine, and started this insane process of rolling out the dough and placing a big slab of butter in the center, then folding the dough over the slab of butter, then rolling the dough out again, and placing another big slab of butter in the center, then folding the dough over the slab of butter, then opening another bottle of wine, then rolling out the dough, and placing another slab of butter in the center, then folding the dough, then drinking more wine, and we got just so so so so giggly and silly and Julia forgot how many times we'd folded-and-slabbed-and-rolled, and then we just started taking photos of our flour- and butter- smeared hands and faces, and at one point I slipped on the butter-greased floor and fell face-forward on the slab of butter, and we couldn't stop laughing...oh, my God, my God, we had so so so much fun...

(She puts the photo back in the drawer and closes it.)

Aren't these drawers just marvelous?

One day I saw these old chests of drawers, a whole wall of them...battered, unloved, unused... *(She's stroking them.)*

...and I had to have them and transform them...and so I pulled out my Platinum Visa card and bought the whole set of them, and then I repainted them…credit is so much fun…

…and I chose a palette of colors that are…well…blue…

…I love blue…

…I love all of the blues, and I wanted to create for the drawers a new life and give each drawer its own identify, but provide for them a…"family" of kindred drawers, so that each would be unique, yet none would be alone. *(She strokes the drawers)*

Let me show you something,

(She opens a drawer, pulls it all the way out, and holds it up to the audience.)

I've lined each drawer.

It's that fun?

I've lined each drawer with a differently, carefully selected paper or cloth or in some cases a collage of cuttings from slick-paged magazines…

Each drawer has its own personality, inhabits its own marvelous little world.

(She replaces the drawer and shuts it.)

And my chairs. Don't you just love them? Aren't they marvelous? I found them one day on the sidewalk, seven of them, old strong soulful weathered distressed unloved and I…I…I identified with them…they were… used and neglected…abandoned and I…I wanted to give them hope… *(She strokes the chairs)*

So I carried them home, one by one, sanded them, repaired them, repainted them…I love blue….and I find it so so so comforting to position them and reposition them and move them next to each other and away from each other…

And I've realized that they have relationships and a shared history, and I love to sit in one chair...

...and then sit in another chair...

...and then move them a bit...

...and sit in a third chair...

...and then move to a fourth chair...

...and then I rearrange them a bit...

...and I sit on a fifth chair...

...and I wonder about who used to sit in the chair? What were the circumstances? Who were the people? What was its history?

(She repositions a chair or two, then sits on one, positions herself just so, and turns to the audience.)

I realize that you recognize the tragedy.

I realize that you've heard the stories, the history, the childhood of deprivation, the persistence, the drive to succeed, the dedicated cultivation of the culinary skills, the gardening skills, the design and marketing skills, the public relations successes, the creation of the persona, the branding, the multi-pronged media crusade, the rise, the beatification, the crisis, the unjust reaction, the fall...

And I had to endure the relentless assaults in the tabloid press and the vicious dissection of my personality on those hideous daytime talk shows hosted by those brain-challenged badly-coiffed outrageously overpaid totally mindless women who sit there all sanctimonious and loose-lipped on their little sofas spreading degrading outrageous unsubstantiated filth about people whom in fact they envy.

And I was called upon repeatedly, due to my mass-audience popularity and the general public's intense interest in every facet of my life, to sit there all lady-

like on the little sofas, and I smiled and nodded and
tilted my head charmingly back and forth, as the
brain-challenged badly-coiffed outrageously overpaid
totally mindless talk-show women asked me about
my regimen of nutritional supplements and colonic
cleansings…

And how I cared for my beautiful flawless skin…

And what I thought of the epidemic of stainless steel
that has invaded American kitchens so that everything
now looks like a giant toaster…

And, of course, they wanted to know about yoga…
because on my nationally syndicated, Emmy-award-
winning conversational-and-self-empowerment
program, I produced an on-going series extoling the
physical and emotional benefits of yoga…

And I demonstrated the downward-facing dog, the
cobra, the triangle…and people loved it, just loved it,
couldn't get enough of it, and many of my fans wanted
me to do a yoga videotape and a yoga how-to book
and a yoga recipe book and a yoga lifestyle book…

And, let me just say right now: I…can't…stand…yoga.

I realize that this is a shocking admission.

But this is exactly the problem when one achieves
stardom: you feel compelled to reshape yourself to be
what your audience demands, denying your true self
to create the person your fans—and I love you—want
you to be…and so I did yoga, and more yoga, and I
hated yoga, and I still hate yoga, and I was miserable.

And I hate bonsai.

…even though I demonstrated bonsai and gushed
endlessly about how I *loved* bonsai and the *beauty* of
bonsai and the *challenge* of bonsai, I absolutely *hate*
bonsai…I mean, why in the fuck don't you just let the
goddamn trees grow the way the want to grow?!

And then they asked me about babies…

…and why I never had babies…

…and didn't I *want* to have babies…

…and why didn't I *adopt* if I couldn't actually *have* babies…

…and I wanted to tell them that it was none of their fucking business, but everything's their business, and if it isn't their business they make it their business, and being a public commodity I was expected to reveal myself and share my humanity to demonstrate that even big and important people like Willa have problems and challenges that are often the same problems and challenges that the little people have, and therefore everyone can just relax and not worry so much because their problems are *just like Willa's.*

I shall now move.

(She moves and poses.)

I shall now move again.

(She crosses to a chair, repositions the chair moving it closer to the audience. She sits and crosses her legs, applies more lipstick, fiddles with her hair, then re-crosses her legs.)

I had not wanted to talk about babies.

(She re-crosses her legs.)

Although as you know for many years I tried to make babies.

And for many years I was tragically unsuccessful at trying to make babies.

Repeated testing using the latest, most sophisticated and expensive diagnostic apparatus revealed that although my ovaries were capable of producing ova, the ova were incomplete ova, lacking necessary genetic

material, the complete complement of proteins to
create a new life.

This was a great heartbreak to me.

And it was a great heartbreak to my dear lovely
mother, now deceased, who so desperately wanted
grandchildren...

And is was a great heartbreak to Summerfield...

...who, despite his many shortcomings, loved children
and wanted to have children, and, as the sensationalist
media has revealed, actually *had* a child, unbeknownst
to me, a secret *"love"* child that he had fathered with a
woman of the lower levels of society during the years
when he was secretly married to me.
(She stops, she fights back tears, she pauses, she recovers.)

I did not know Summerfield was sexaholic.

I had not been told.

Everyone else knew he was sexaholic. *You* probably
knew he was sexaholic.

I should have known.

I should have suspected.

The excuses, the mumbled phone calls, the nights and
there were more and more of them when he never
came home, and I lay awake sobbing, desperate...

I was the one who had the income, let us understand
that.

I was the one who had the reputation, the press, the
adoring fans, people stopping me in the street to say,
"We love you, Willa. We love the way you wear your
hair. We love the way you screwed the IRS." People
who have stood by me during the good years, the
controversial years, the long years during my climb to
the top, and people cried out my name, and asked for

my autograph, my 8-by-10, and wrote me asking for advice....

I shall open a drawer.

(She opens a drawer, looks, then stops.)

Medical marijuana is very important to me.

Medical marijuana is the issue.

(She takes out a parcel of tightly wrapped joints, tied with a ribbon.)

There were many years before I discovered medical marijuana and they were very painful years and the years now are still painful but with the help of medical marijuana I have learned to deal with the pain, in fact, even *enjoy* the pain.

(She pulls out a joint from the packet of joints, rolls it lovingly between her fingers, smells it, savors it, then lights the joint and takes a drag, holds it, then exhales.)

One of the things that's so beautiful about medical marijuana is the fact that though the various "clubs" you can purchase a wide variety of blends, including a range of Hawaiian, Chilean, and Californian hybrids, the "Purple Kush", the "Blue Virgin", the "Train Wreck".

(She takes another drag, holds it, then exhales.)

I just find it so so so relaxing to ingest an appropriately prescribed quantity of quality all-organic pesticide-free medical marijuana and experience its ameliorative effects... *(She takes another drag, holds it, then exhales.)* I have a marvelous doctor, adore the man, marvelous, beautiful, compassionate man, he understands, cares, realizes the stresses that attend celebrity and the active bold-faced life style.

(She sets the joint down, collects herself.)

Where were we?

(She thinks a bit.)

It was something important, wasn't it... It was something about...

Sometimes I find that medical marijuana helps put things into a more...*appropriate* perspective.

Sometimes we think that that the things that we're thinking about are very important things, very critically complicated things, yet so often we learn that the things we're thinking about are just things that we're thinking about, and beyond that they aren't much at all.

(She stands crosses to a drawer, opens it, and pulls out a bag of Oreos. She takes an Oreo and returns and sits.)

I understand the little people.

(She takes a bite of the Oreo.)

I understand the little people because my own people were themselves little people and I was a little people.

(She takes another bite of the Oreo.)

And then I became a big people.

(She eats the rest of the Oreo.)

And I had a big life filled with big people and big events and big houses, but at heart I am a little people who knows and feels deeply about the beautiful little people.

We're all little people.

With little needs and little hopes and little fantasies...

Of course I trusted Summerfield!

I *married* Summerfield!

He managed the accounts, he managed the business, he was the financial know-it-all, the merger-and-acquisitions know-it-all, the get-around-the-trademarks

know-it-all, and I didn't know that he was parking the
money in some illegal off-shore tax shelter...I signed
the papers, he told me to sign the papers, I signed the
papers because I always signed the papers, and when
the I R S blew the whistle, and the justice department
blew the whistle, and the sensationalist butt-sniffing
media flew into a frenzy of self-righteous picture-
taking, smut-peddling...it was *my* name on the papers,
my signature on the papers, and *my* illegal off-shore tax
shelter, and I was vilified.

And during the trial, which cost me what I had left of
my capital and my dignity, the fact that Summerfield
and I were married became an issue, and the
separation became an issue, and the divorce became an
issue, and Summerfield's love-child with the slut from
Wal-Mart became an issue, and everything was my
fault. *I* was the immoral one, *I* was the dishonest one,
I was the one who was responsible for the business, *I*
was the one who couldn't control her husband, *I* was
the one who couldn't *keep* her husband, *I* was the one
who'd been loved and adored, and now I was public
filth!

I shall now open a drawer.

*(She opens a drawer, looks in it, lets out a shriek of horror.
Closes the drawer...opens it, shrieks...closes it.)*

It is important to confront the horror.

(She opens the drawer, looks in it again, shrieks, closes it.)

We have to acknowledge the horror, embrace the
horror.

I have tried to capture all of the horrors, all of the
demons, and I have placed each of them in a drawer.

(Opens a drawer just a bit, but doesn't look in)

Here I have collected cruelty. My own cruelty, the
cruelty of others, the wounds of cruelty, the indelible

scars, the searing pain, and I have wrapped it all up
in a beautifully simple indigo blue cloth, scented with
sage and cedar, and put it away and shut the drawer.

(Opens a drawer just a bit, but doesn't look in)

Here I have collected violence and hate. I have
gathered the violence I've committed, the violence
I've endured, my hate, and the hate of the world, and
I have wrapped them up in a neutral organic material,
silky but not shiny, a pale, unthreatening mauve,
scented with a hint of thyme and eucalyptus, and put it
all away and shut the drawer.

(Opens a drawer just a bit, but doesn't look in)

Here is envy…

(Another drawer)

Here is rejection…

And I confess that sometimes late at night I like to open
the drawer of rejection…

*(She looks into the drawer, and takes out a nicely wrapped
little package of rejection.)*

I like to take rejection out and feel it. Smell it. Handle
it. Turn it over. And over.

I love rejection…so beautiful…so tranquil…so final…
so sad.

No matter how much you try, how worthy you are,
how much you love and give, you will still suffer
rejection again and again, hurt again, vilified again…
stripped…naked…vulnerable…trembling…

(She places rejection back in the drawer and closes it.)

I shall now move.

*(She crosses to a chair, pulls it closer to the audience, the
sits.)*

As I have shared with you, my dear dear mother, now deceased, was an orphan.

She and her baby sister Ramona were abandoned and left to die, but were narrowly rescued by the authorities who placed them in an orphanage where they were raised.

It was a horror.

My mother bore the scars.

A lifetime of depression bathed in alcohol…

…a loveless, short-lived marriage…

…and she and her sister Ramona, now deceased, had a fatal falling out, and they never spoke to each other again.

Tormented by insecurities, my poor dear dear mother never had the opportunity to learn how to cook or acquire basic homemaking skills.

And so as a little girl—and, as you know, I was an only child—it was necessary for me to be my *own* mother as well as being my *mother's* mother and learn to bake and sew and baste the turkey and make the jello and beat the egg whites and scour the sink and wash the windows and wash the clothes and the towels and the sheets and iron the blouses and hem the skirts and mop the floor and defrost the refrigerator and sanitize the bathroom and fertilize the roses and mow the lawn and trim the hedge and deal with the weeds and the crab grass and the banana slugs and do the grocery shopping and call the plumber and stand up to the bill collectors. And I loved it. Loved it. Just loved it. Absolutely loved loved loved it. And I planted bulbs and made new curtains and repainted the living room and filled the house with African violets and maiden hair ferns and I hung the sheets outside to dry on the line to get that fresh wonderful sun-scented feel of clean clean clean…and I knew that it would be my calling.

And so at school I started sharing my knowledge and experience during show-and-tell, and then my teachers asked me to demonstrate some basic cooking and cleaning strategies, and, although I was liked, more-or-less, by the other students, I wasn't really very popular, mostly rejected by the boys, resented by the girls, and I never, you know, *dated*. I mean, none of the boys were like, you know, *interested* in me, and, of course, I was the one who catered all of the parties and the proms, and the homecomings, and the football celebrations, I did the decorations, and the décor, and selected the music, and made the food and the punch, and did the clean up, and although I did attain a measure of respect based on my homemaking skills and precocious early adulthood, I was never, you know, really *accepted*.

And so early on I became determined to expand my knowledge and skills and dedicate myself to ennobling the role of the homemaker and to help the homemaker to take pride in her role and excel in her role, and by creating a beautiful environment and serving nutritious beautifully-presented meals help to create a beautiful world.

And it was then that my true identity was born. And I became "Willa". Just "Willa". Exclusively "Willa", the one, the only, the goddess of the home and the fulfilling life style.

I didn't know what sex was.

My mother didn't tell me.

I don't think she actually knew.

And, I mean, okay, alright, I had a little sort of idea, I mean I listened to the girls giggling in the locker room and knew that there was something going on that I wasn't a part of, but I was hopelessly naïve, and although I had stirrings, deep mysterious longings and whisperings of desire, it wasn't until Summerfield, seriously, Summerfield, before any man expressed any real desire for me. I mean, there were flirtations, and improper, shall we say, *propositions*, and occasionally someone would ask me out, usually someone who wanted a mother... And when Summerfield began courting me, showering me with gifts and attention, I was instantly infatuated, and, of course, this was well after I had become famous and wealthy, and yet I was so simple and trusting and inexperienced that it didn't occur to me that his motives might have been something other than honorable.

(Suddenly tearful) I had to beg Summerfield for sex.

I bathed, I moisturized, I scented, I seduced, on my knees...at first...he wanted, he needed, he devoured me, loved me...and then...

...and then...

He was tired...he wasn't feeling very well...the estimated tax payments, the N B A finals, calls from other women, the nights I was left alone, humiliated, mortified...

(She stops to wipe tears...)

Orgasm was not the issue.

And for many of you, and I understand this, you have told me many many many times that orgasm *is* the issue. So many lovely, heartfelt letters you've written me—and I love you—about your desire for orgasm, your need for orgasm, your obsession about achieving a mind-numbing, life-changing, love-filled, violently gut-wrenching, hallucinogenic, eye-poppingly transformative orgasm.

And although I have achieved orgasm...

...from time to time...

...not every time, but, I mean...well...I've never been
what you would call wholly "orgasmic" ...I mean, I
don't have anything *against* orgasm, exactly, but...
it's not, you know...I mean, I have always preferred
the, you know, *foreplay* aspects...the lowering of the
lights...the candles...the soft, yet throbbing music...the
tentative touching, the tender kissing, the not so tender
kissing, the fumbling, gradual disrobing, tongue,
hands, moving through the liturgy of arousal, the
tumescence, the breathing, the moaning, the secretions,
the urgency of copulation, the intensity, the vital
essential raw terrifying scream of desire... *(She is quite
aroused, then calming herself)*.

Summerfield could not achieve orgasm.

With me, that is.

Apparently he could achieve the appropriately
expected ejaculatory response with *other* women, more
subservient, less discriminating women who were not
threatening to him, by virtue of their inferior intellect
and big-haired sensibilities...but with me.... *(Tears
up)* We tried...for years we tried...different positions,
techniques, rhythms, with music, without music, with
light, without light...it was exhausting...

I had never realized that there were men who could
not achieve orgasm, women yes, so many of you, and I
love you, have written me about your frustrations over
not being able to attain a brain-blasting state of erotic
spasm, your fear that you aren't fully female, aren't
really all woman in the deep, deep, gut-centered, all
devouring, all encompassing, Angelina Jolie kind of
way...

But *men*...I thought that men were relentlessly,
efficiently programmed and driven to orgasm, the
bursting forth of all their little repressed outrage as

they desperately attempt to overcome their in-born heartfelt sense of cosmic impotence.

Men are so tragic, really, aren't they?

I mean, I love men, I mean, some men, I mean, most of them are okay, and I realize that many of you here tonight are of the masculine affiliation and I feel so much compassion for you.

It must be so very truly deeply painfully difficult being a man. All those requirements...expectations... demands...you have to be strong, you have to be brave, you have to be decisive, gentle, caring, commanding but not intimidating, powerful but not dominating, know how to throw a ball, fix the plumbing, fix the car, sharpen the axe, use the axe, start the fire, put out the fire, hold everything together when everything's falling apart, while constantly dealing with little wifey's passive-aggressive hysteria and temperamental needs and whiney disposition.

And you have that little ugly tube of skin hanging between your legs...

And it must be so humiliating.

(Beat)

Summerfield had a tragically small penis...

...a little stinky, shriveled thing...and he was so proud of it...liked to show it off...and I'd tell him how thrilling it was and it wasn't thrilling...

...and this is part of the problem that women spend so much time having to tell men how thrilling their stinky little dick is and then men believe it because they're desperate to believe it...

And I've seen many. Well, not that many...I mean, well, okay...quite a number...

...because when you're in my position and widely loved and admired, a lot of men, an amazing number, if fact, come up to you and want to show you their dick...

...I mean, it's sort of nice, quite sweet really that they would want to pull out their stinky little thing and wave it at me...and I've always tried to be...you know...complimentary...and say something...you know...positive...even though there's usually nothing very positive to say.

And sometimes, just to be nice, I ask them if they've given the little fella a name...and an astonishing number of men, in fact, *have*...Roscoe's quite popular...

...and sometimes I wonder why men don't just wave their little things at each other and leave women out of it, since really most women are more interested in personality, and sense of humor, and intoxicating body odor, and luxurious hair, and luxurious income.

I shall now move.

(She moves and poses.)

I shall now move again.

(She moves and poses.)

I shall open a drawer.

(She opens a drawer and takes out a bottle of Bombay Sapphire gin, opens it and takes a deep swig, starts to re-cap it, but then takes another big swig, then recaps the bottle. Then turning to the audience.)

After the separation, the divorce, the relentless publicity about Summerfield's series of romances with women with increasingly bouffant hairdos...

...and the exposé of my tempestuous lesbian love affair with the ex-wife of the disgraced ex-Senator...

...after the cancellation of my television show...

...the tawdry business about my alleged shoplifting...

...the series of incidents involving my public intoxication...

...the personal mortification of my butchered chin lift...

I retreated from the tyranny of day-to-day exposure.

I cut my hair, colored my hair, disguised myself with scarves and hats and dark glasses and walked the streets as an outsider, unobserved, anonymous, lost...

...and I was prescribed a "cocktail" of prescription drugs to help me deal with the anxiety, fear, paranoia...

...which numbed my perceptions and compromised my ability to balance, and I became easily disoriented and fell as I was getting out of the cab and someone recognized me and the sensationalist media was there on the spot, camera ready, the evening news, flash!, the screaming headlines, flash!, the picture of me, arm reaching out to catch myself as I fell to the pavement...

And this is what people want. This is what people want.

This is what you want, isn't it?

This is what you're looking for....the nasty little exposé, the soiled linen? This is why you've come here tonight, isn't it, to savor a little tabloid filth?

And they're following me, hidden microphones, hidden cameras, I'm serious, encircling me, watching me right this moment, a continual real-time twitter feed of every transaction, every sigh, every tear, and some of you, I'm serious, right here, look around, some of you are members of the media underground, disguised, look around, sitting here, look around, seemingly benign and friendly, but here to torment me...

(She stomps around a bit.)

God is upset.

(She stomps around some more.)

God is so very very upset.

(She stomps around even more.)

(Then grateful) God is such a beautiful God, and he has been reassuring me that no matter how hopeless it all seems, and how lost I may feel...

He's been leaving me little messages...

I put them away carefully in a drawer, beautiful personal love notes from God that I cherish and read and reread and find solace in God's love and care.

(She opens a drawer, takes out a pile of love notes, takes one, opens it, reads it silently, is moved, then...)

(Reading) What you do is insignificant, because you are insignificant.

(She smiles, folds the note back up carefully, places it back in the pile, takes another one, opens it, then...)

(Reading) There is no "you". You do not exist. Only I exist.

(She smiles, folds the note back up carefully, places it back in the pile, takes another one, opens it, then...)

(Reading) People who choose to identify themselves by only one name will die a slow, painful, and agonizing death; only God can have one name.

(She smiles, folds the note back up carefully, places it back in the pile, and places the pile of notes back in the drawer and closes it.)

Religion is so comforting, don't you think?

I just adore religion, so mysterious, all-encompassing,
humbling...and when I was in the spotlight, obsessed
with the climb to the top, I forgot about religion
because I became infatuated with style, and décor
became the issue, color and texture and thread-count
became the issue...I love textiles, I adore textiles, I
don't want you to think that just because I reconnected
with religion that I abandoned textiles, or abandoned
my appreciation of hand-crafted cheeses, or Italian
shoes...

(She takes another swig of gin.)

It's so difficult being human.

So many pressures, expectations, and we get ourselves
all knotted up and tormented about who we are and
who we should be and what we think we have to
do, and, when we are young we think we have to be
happy, and we set about to do the things that we think
we need to do to be happy, and we achieve the things
we think we have to achieve in order to be happy...

I achieved.

Achievement is over-rated.

I achieved because I was insecure and I thought that if
I achieved I'd be secure.

But you can't just achieve, because once you achieve,
people expect you to achieve, and you have to keep
on achieving, and you have to achieve more, and you
have to achieve more, and you have to achieve more,
and pretty soon it's all just achieve achieve achieve,
and then you look down at your pile of achievement
and realize that you're more alone and insecure than
you ever were.

(She takes another swig of gin.)

Could I help it if I was irresistible?

Could I help it if people wanted to be with me, talk to me, listen to me, imitate me, touch me, name their daughters after me, *be* me?

It was very stressful.

The responsibility was overwhelming…

…people expecting me to have the answers, to comfort them, inspire them…

….and everyone wants a story…

…a tidy little narrative, predictable cause-and-effect, all uplifting and sensible and comforting and reassuring…

So I tried to create a story…

…and provide uplift…

…and perpetuate the myth that life is a nice little narrative, and that I was the go-to expert on living a life that's fulfilling and beautiful—how to set the table for maximum impact, how to nourish your mitochondria to support robust health, how to leverage minimal talents into a position of social influence and fame.

But I didn't know shit!

I never knew shit.

I still don't know shit.

And I sought to convince everybody that I *did* know shit, but it was a lie…life is just events, and the events don't make sense, and we don't even control the events, the events control us, but nobody wants to hear that, and so I couldn't say that, and so I desperately tried to perpetuate the lie, but at some point I just couldn't lie any more, I couldn't do anything any more…

(She moves a chair, then moves another chair, then repositions the first chair then sits, and puts on lipstick, then crosses her legs.)

Then in a moment of great loneliness...I was staring out the window, watching the rain, obsessively picking at my nails...Summerfield called.

He wanted to talk, just say "hi", said he was worried about me, had heard the stories, was concerned, missed me, had been thinking about me, and then he asked me if I'd like to meet him for dinner at the little fish place we liked down by the docks...

I had misgivings, I wasn't sure, I said I shouldn't, I said I should, I said "why not," I knew it was a mistake, I was worried about what to wear, I was worried about being seen, after all I'd been through, the public humiliation, the emotional torment...

We both wore dark glasses...

And we had a couple of cocktails and the fried calamari with the nice lemon-wasabi dipping sauce... he looked tired, older, you get to know a person, you can see in their eyes a kind of...loss...

And after a few pleasantries, catching up about what was going on with old friends, some harmless reminiscing, a laugh or two about getting old, he began rubbing his foot slowly, lovingly along my leg and I placed my hand on his beautiful massive masculine thigh...

So many of you have been in a similar situation, haven't you?

So many of you have been torn by the conflicting emotions of...

Love is so confusing.

I am terrified of desire, I am thrilled by desire...

I have placed desire in a drawer and I have taken
desire out of the drawer, I have placed desire back in
the drawer...

I had not wanted to see him....

...you have to understand...

...my heart had been broken...

...and I knew I shouldn't meet him, see him again,
touch him...

And he told me how much he missed me, and how
stupid he'd been for fooling around with other women,
and how I was the only one, and how he dreamed
about me and desired me and loved me and needed
me...

...and at one point I leaned in to him and we started
to engage in a gentle tongue kiss...a lovely lingering
sweet soulful slow yet passionate rubbing of tongue
on tongue, lips pressed to lips, losing ourselves in the
beauty of the moment, the beauty of love and desire....

...when suddenly a singularly scummy sensationalist-
media paparazzo who was at the table next to us,
snapped a photo, and Summerfield rose to confront
him...

I ran from the restaurant in tears of humiliation...

The next day the picture...

...it was horrifying...

...sensationalist headlines: "Willa and Summerfield's
Secret Rendezvous!", the photo of "THE KISS," the
snarky commentary, the heartless remarks...

...and they noted that although I looked radiant, I had
gained considerable weight, and of course I'd gained
considerable weight...the stress, the fried calamari...

The horror of being a celebrity.

Every wrinkle, every crease, every pound, every time you change the color of your hair or show some cleavage.

And I started getting the letters of outrage, people upset that I would meet again with Summerfield after...

I've only wanted to help people.

That has always been my only motivation.

I love people.

I see their need, I feel their...anxiety...there is so much anxiety...

And then a week later there was a picture of Summerfield with some redhead and her seventeen-inch waist snuggling together at the *very same* restaurant.

I despise Summerfield! I always despised Summerfield!

I loved Summerfield and I despised Summerfield... love/despise, love/despise, despised him because I loved him, caught in the conflict that deep emotion provokes...

I shall now move

(She moves and poses.)

I shall now open a drawer.

(She crosses and opens the Patsy Cline drawer and sings:)

Two cigarettes in an ashtray,
My love and I in a small cafe...

(Then speaking)

Then another woman came along and stole her love away.

(She tears up.)

...I dreamed about Patsy, I was just a child, I sent her love letters, I wanted to protect her, keep her safe... Patsy had alcohol issues, I have alcohol issues, not like really big alcohol issues, but, you know....

(She closes the drawers, takes another swig of gin, then another.)

As you know, because the flagrantly inflammatory tabloid press informed you, that after the authorities found me wandering the streets disheveled and delusional, they had me institutionalized.

And the team of therapists who treated me took everything away from me, my clothes, my shoes, my lipstick...they said that I couldn't use lipstick any more and I tried to explain that lipstick was an essential part of my identity, but they wanted me to erase my identity and start over.

(She applies more lipstick.)

And then they said that I had a self-destructive obsessive-compulsive complex.

And I said that *everyone* has a self-destructive obsessive-compulsive complex, that life *itself* is a self-destructive obsessive-compulsive complex.

And then they said that my self-destructive obsessive-compulsive behaviors were the *wrong* self-destructive obsessive-compulsive behaviors and that I need to develop new, more *self-affirming* self-destructive obsessive-compulsive behaviors, and let me just say right now that the alleged professionals who were making these statements were all about a third my age...naïve, immature, overly educated post-adolescents with no life experience whatsoever.

And then they told me that I didn't have an integrated personality, that personality was the issue, that identity was the issue, and that identity is a syndrome, each of us is a syndrome, a set of self-destructive obsessive-compulsive characteristics and behaviors, I am the Willa syndrome, and you are the You syndrome, and we're trapped in our syndrome...

And now I'm disintegrating.

I can't multi-task any more.

I can't remember anymore...what I just said, what I ate last night, names are gone, faces are disappearing, events occur and dissolve...

(Suddenly a drawer slides opens on its own, and smoke begins to pour out. She gasps and rushes to the drawer and slams it shut and holds it.)

Please don't look.

It's the media.

It's awful.

Coming through the door, the windows, slipping in through the cracks, little cameras focused to record my private moments...

(Another drawer opens on its own, and smoke begins to pour out.)

Don't look, please don't look.

(She rushes over to close the drawer.)

Following me every moment, trying to capture the embarrassments, the insults, the humiliations, pandering to the public's self-destructive obsessive-compulsive need for controversy and outrage....

(Suddenly furious, screaming) Vultures. Vultures! Vultures! *(Pointing at the audience)* I've seen you, eyeing the smut-filled tabloids at the check out, pausing to assess the cover, see who's life they're trying to destroy for your amusement, gloating, laughing, feeling your

little sanctimonious self-satisfaction, your little self-centered sense of superiority… Vultures!

You're here to laugh at me, aren't you, ridicule me strip me, expose me…

You want to see my underwear don't you, you want to sniff it don't you, that's what you're here for isn't, pretending you love me, care about me, need me, and all you want is to view the dirty linen, *(Opening a drawer,)* …here, here, I'll show you, *(Exhibits/tosses out underpants)* you want to see my lingerie, look for the holes, look for the incriminating stains…get a good whiff, here, here, look at it, here, look at it, see, see, you want to smell…. Smell it! Smell it!

…after all I've done for you, all the fucking cookies I baked, all the fucking homemaking tips I shared, the decorating ideas, the self-improvement advice, the can't-miss investment strategies… Voyeuristic vultures! Spending money to come see a disintegrating old lady show you her underwear… *(Opening her skirt)* Want to see my underpants? Want to see my underpants? See! Look! See! That's what you wanted isn't it? Isn't it? Are you happy? Don't you realize what you've done? You've destroyed me! Sucked my soul! I used to have a soul, a beautiful soul and then you sucked it, sucked me dry! Soul suckers! This is what you've done to me. See? Happy? *(Raging around the stage)* Don't mess with me! Don't mess with me! Don't think you can destroy me! Soul suckers! Fucking soul suckers! Cannibalistic blood-sucking soul suckers!

(Long pause, as she tearfully tries to collect herself, calm herself.)

(Tearfully) I shall now move.

(She makes an attempt to move, but can't.)

I shall now move.

(She makes an attempt to move, but can't.)

I shall now move.

(She moves haltingly.)

I shall now move.

(She moves haltingly then stomps around a bit and poses.)

I shall now sit.

(She crosses to a chair, pulls it closer to the audience, then sits. She very haphazardly and defiantly applies more lipstick, vastly exceeding the outline of her lips—a child-like smear of red. Then she crosses to a drawer, opens it, takes out a joint, crosses back to the chair, sits positioning herself very precisely, lights the joint, inhales deeply, then exhales.)

It was destined that we would come together tonight.

We've been together before...you feel that, don't you...

There is a deep deep unspoken symbiotic bond between us...

...a shared sense of...loss...of strength...of survival...

I shall open a drawer.

(She stands crosses, and opens a drawer.)

(Announces)

Miss Patsy Cline.

(She sings:)

I fall to pieces,
Each time I see you again...

(She fight back tears and closes the drawer and turns to the audience.)

I'm so honored you wanted to be with me tonight.

I wanted to be with you.

I love you.

I need you.

I don't exist without you.

You don't need me, I know that, I know that...you don't need me at all...I tried to make you believe that you needed me, tried to seduce you into loving me...

That's all I wanted. Just love.

Please let me leave you with something beautiful.

(She crosses to a drawer, opens it, and takes out a set of old account ledgers.)

After Aunt Ramona died...breast cancer, double mastectomy, remission, metastasis, death...

I was called upon to clean out her things...

She was my mother's sister, never close, never saw each other, rarely spoke, my mother wouldn't talk about her, I barely, just barely knew her, met her for lunch a time or two, always immaculately dressed, always wearing gloves, very reserved, refined, aloof, yet gracious...terrifyingly alone.

I found a meticulous arrangement...

...a Shaker simplicity...

...minimal possessions...

...very few things, but very beautiful things...

...a few silk blouses hung just so, a few cotton blouses with little appliqués hung just so, lovely lace hankies, lovely silk and wool scarves...a stenographer, never married, happily single, a quiet spinsterhood of reading and attending lectures on ornithology and anything Baroque...

...an immaculately simple beautifully controlled aesthetic life...

(Showing the account ledgers) These are her cash accounts. *(She fights back tears.)* Every day...every

item…every expenditure recorded in meticulous detail…

… *(Reading)* Groceries, five dollars and seventy-five cents…batteries for smoke detector, one dollar and seventy cents… *(Tearing up)* yarn, three dollars and sixty-five cents… *(Overcome, she closes the ledger)* And she saved…*saved*, do you remember savings? …each month…her little dollars and little cents…and she bought savings bonds, United States government savings bonds, series E…

And gloves… *(She opens another drawer takes out gloves)* thirty-two pairs of gloves, thirty-two pairs… *(She holds up the gloves and shows them, and lays them out fanned across the floor.)* She was of the era when a woman did not leave the home unless she was wearing gloves…thirty-two pairs, all colors, spring, summer, fall, winter…Aunt Ramona's own little obsessive-compulsive indulgence, isn't that lovely, one little mad wild beautiful wonderfully crazy extravagance, in an otherwise carefully measured life of restraint and simplicity…

…32 pairs of gloves…small…perfect…beautiful…

(She picks up one pair gloves, and holds them lovingly to her breast.)

(Blackout)

END OF PLAY

www.ingramcontent.com/pod-product-compliance
Lightning Source LLC
Chambersburg PA
CBHW070035110426
42741CB00035B/2785